T0361662

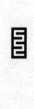

she is the earth

flood editions, chicago

she
is
the
earth

ali

cobby

eckermann

This volume appears under license from

Magabala Books Aboriginal Corporation in Australia

Published by Flood Editions in 2024

www.floodeditions.com

ISBN 979-8-9857874-5-0

Design and composition by Crisis

Printed on acid-free, recycled paper in Canada

First North American Edition

to all who have endured extreme loss
and especially the women
who walked beside me
who taught the freedom of nature
and how to honour her song

she
is
the
earth

and so it begins
a new beginning
not quite genesis

yidaki is vibrating
mourning evolving
the epic carries me
unfixed unformed

my body unknown
I am out of tune
a need to belong
debases me

liberate me
to the cycle of life
refrain my desire
guide my heart

everything is fluid
as I drift apart

the seed of origin
I cannot remain

across warm water
a memory of home

in this emergence
wholeness is fluid

across dark water
I see emptiness

a salty scent
I can taste it

within this world
I am embalmed

I float on a sliver
of amniotic fluid
across a plateau
that has no end

only breathing
defines me
there is solace
in this ennui

I am lukewarm
and irriguous
all my senses
inconversable

time suspends
survival shakes
yidaki respires
an illusion

the path of life
is narrowing
in this isolation
my body subsides

I am amnesia
I am foetal
faceless I dream
a remnant of me

exhausted I am
unable to breathe
I scratch for air
my mouth a cave

and I resound
an agent of sight
a ricochet of life
pleading for love

intuition lands
as coldness cracks

the path is fading
running out of time

and I must run
as water laps
I am a land bridge
about to drown

a fog descends
I enter alone
all is reduced
in off-white air

in neutrality
there is no vision
outlines erased
I float unmade

my heart is abyssal
with pelagic blood
I am unconceived
yet wanting

in opaqueness
a hint of self
I flow freely
animate within

in the opaqueness
I glimpse whitecaps

surging towards me
at shoulder height

frigid I stand
awaiting impact

the frothy streaks
bubble and foam

yet never reach
a consternation

what is a threshold
if not a memory
I exist here
ready to enter
the door is closed

as thought subdues
keys appear in my eyes
admission is an opera
the crescendo of breath
is flight and I am away

my heartbeats echo
rapid the sound of fear

atmosphere encloses
I am conjoined to sky

the pantomime is brutal
an organism gulping air

ventilating distinctive
my mouth forms a bubble

forcing air into lungs
I float on breath

inhaling hovers me
I seek revival

in silence is blankness
a creation without birth
even nature is absent

the vacancy of flora
is a starkness endured
as if a slaughter

the truancy of fauna
is a separation endured
as if a beheading

the void in my heart
listens for any vow
for the inclusion of me

my scream is silent
yet reverberates
around the world

the sky and the sea
are defining of blue

suspended on water
I paddle through time

I strain to expand
an inception of self

on the horizon afar
air and ocean greet

as if breathing now
the water is tidal

a kiss of life ripples
in the depths below

I have obtained
a promise of earth

entrapped by exploration
I am between worlds

my day is not the evening
nor the dawn

the wind is not my breath
the stillness not my stare

neither a grimace
nor a smile

I am an empty chamber
reverberating inside

the land bridge ends
I am submerged

my skin saturates
flaking its weight

foreboding sinks me
I see black rocks below

as I am floundering
one rock turns turtle

it gathers me
rides me ashore

I crawl over pebbles
clinging to life

I become lichen
softness on harsh

beyond the rocks
a tectonic song

an aural trance
movement surreal

exhausted I lie sodden
my cheek rests on soft sand

I watch light bend over water
a mirage melds with landscape

across grains of sand on a windswept dune
the mirage is risen from humankind

lifting my head I see dimension
my eyes squint to focus this truth

the mirage is beckoning me
she is zircon and shimmering

blues and yellows fuse to fact
I realise she is my mother

her scent is water and earth
I cry for nourishment

longing for touch like metaphoric rock
I am bound by the lure of crusade

low rocks black and braille
transform a tangible promise

I see an image of a child
it is a faint mirror of me

I conceive a girl out of want
naming gender out of need

I mouth her name Blessing
she will be my sanctity

a notion of existence
without her I am alone

aloneness
separated
inadequate

respiration
acceptance
decisionless

sensations
meditation
benevolence

please come
please guide
please heal

I enter
turgid
alone

in a dream
dinosaur birds

sickle claws
grab at me

I bleed
lime clay

I purge
all ire

beyond the rocks
the trance is aural

a sonic of shale
a textural silt

tumbling shaping
a primordial dance

despite the risk
a solace sound

mud stone is surreal
plankton and quartz

unseen the tidal
gravitates nearby

despite instability
firmness begins

I am tantamount
an inception of self

a heartbeat born
a spectrum restores

it is the embrace
heaven and earth

I walk distorted
less sway
less grace

I talk distorted
less smile
less safe

I pray distorted
what to
who with

in distance I hear her
pattering of feet

ankle deep in water
bridging terra firma

I push towards her
eager in effort

reborn in purpose
I am midway

when I approach
she disappears

my question exhales
audibly before me

I lie down giving
.myself to the world

troubled afraid
peace eludes me

my desire to belong
humiliates me

above a faint orb hangs
a half-moon portrays

sun and moon and sky
I witness the miracle

when a heart feels joy
the sky turns sunrise

my hands lift to shade
my eyes from the glare

along the horizon
soft hues rotate

my life is awakening
crimson and orange

inflating gratitude
I stretch my limbs

warmth on my skin
breath turns to fog

a swelling of breath
the upsurge is flight

from nowhere
a bird calls

amplified
it is terrible

startled
I stumble

spilling
drifting

the air flutters
an irresolute state

the sun is birthing
a shadow of me

my shadow tugs me
away from the sun

temptation to stay
is so appealing

my shadow sprints away
attached I too must flee

we hurry in unison
we hurry in urgency

lemon streaks the sky
as the sun peers at us

the sun is rising
my shadow shrinking

as the sun zeniths
my shadow vanishes

as the sun peaks
I debark my past

commit my essence
a lifetime quest

my haste is futile
Blessing stays beyond

she is an isthmus
I remain cervix

I find a strand of hair
turned garnet by the sun
an incandescent sign

she resumes the horizon
unaware of my presence
she is resounding

her feet form imprints
slow shallows that swirl
a starfish maze

I am bound to her
she is my lineage
the mark of revival

a new cadence alights
I scope perspective

the sound of her
is a constant

I continue to follow
the promise of her

breath and breadth
reduce remoteness

I dream of the mother
she builds a bough shelter
collects skulls now bleached
the dream of warning

tied to twirl on the breeze
when a storm appears
the skulls knock together
it is the sound of dread

like metamorphic rock
black mica refuses to yield
I tiptoe through a silent world
cocooned with imagination

planting myself in her
within her footprints
my soles are reality
lacerated and bloody

a gentle light
is refracting

a gentle light
is soaring

a gentle light
is in orbit

a gentle light
is the embryo

once fissured
I feel my future

despite my quest
there is no bond

only a moment
of absolute trust

only a moment
of awkward choice

only a moment
defying the odds

my overglance
an instinctive view

rocks reappear
black stark

a jagged reality
against the unseen

sporadic they form
a direction

I am relieved
guided now

in my heart
doubt is halted

the beach is artwork
a seaside gallery

along this observatory
is the blueprint of birds

aquatic and thermal
their voice the canvas

against undying blue
flocks form moving mist

I roam over middens
white dunes and flats

it is a moment of praise
when pebbles turn frog

this chorus salvation
observe it

I find a feather
frail and defined
I draw it to me

yearning I study
the web of vanes
a map of promise

calling loudly to her
on the fusion of rachis
I seek a message

I need you I need you
I trust you I trust you
the feather vibrates

a need to belong
craves definition

reckless I recline
arching my back

as light flecks fuse
a rainbow appears

as colours burst
hemispheres open

I become equinox
the path of the sun

my skin turns brown
I become seasonal

the world revolving
as my mind evolves

at sunset my mouth opens
mute vigorous stretched

as darkness sets
pessimism prevails

footsteps unseen
lead to nowhere

in this blackness
fear flecks flash

eyes unsure
open or closed

red and blue
atoms of light

pulsing red
starry blue

open or closed
mind unsure

gulls strobe
into my mouth

ingesting all
angst reduces

suspended in time
the world is flat

the horizon rising
to my eye level

Blessing remains
on the horizon

in our reflection
she seems closer

and I am calmed
almost belonging

we become visible
to each other

yonder she dances
with a full moon

within this umbra
I am eclipsed

as Blessing diminishes
she sleeps with the moon

when the moon wanes
they laugh together

so far far away
yet inside me

humbly emerged
I raise my eyes

in the ether above
I hear singing

my ears strain
to learn the song

my neck strains
to retain the view

in this phantom state
time is transparent

from behind the moon
a shadow form flies

a silhouette of an owl
its wings surround me

the ground turns neon
as the owl swoops down

my aura is shifting
observing listening

dark eyes hold me
I am mesmerised

the owl is talking
the owl is teaching

I learn the night
I learn the journey

in astute twilight
a magpie arrives

monotypic
black and white

landing at her feet
Blessing knows it

bending to stroke it
it nudges her hand

high pitched complex
neither shows fear

intrigued I slide
decided I crawl

evidence of life
is the panorama

I am peripheral
I am cusping life

as I scurry to them
an illusion begins

the bird appears
larger in size

am I nearing
is it growing

the question remains
without resentment

without understanding
perception is fraught

dawn is cerebral
my mind consumed

bird and Blessing
are hand in hand

transformed now
human and human

a flood plain greets
an energy of sound

they dance on air
dainty and assured

ripples around me
surge me forward

in a cooking pot
I stare at salt

adding water
I pray for food

hungry now
I drink the ocean

at the base of a tree
I uncover a stone

it resembles an owl
I place it by my fire

the rock sings to me
as salt water boils

there is no food
it offers feathers

in fire smoke
I am animate

fish beckon me
from the water

birds beckon me
from the air

animals beckon me
from the earth

in fire smoke
I am reviving

I am fire now
I have medicine

I am recalling
all I have known

I am releasing
all I have hoarded

I am seeking
all I have dreamed

dreams appear
vibrant in the night

the dreams reappear
viscous in the day

dreams are a promise
dreams are a compass

as song fills air
it is a hymn

as dew seals sand
it is a rebirth

emotions flow
on firmer ground

the drama
is brutal

unable to grieve
unable to sing

I am exhausted
tearful grounding

I am pelican
gulping air

I remove my tongue
plant it in the ground
savour the blood

muteness is a gift
it is wise to wait
relearn to speak

clarity of my eyes
the sand dunes
are seducing me

luring me to remain
distracting venture
preventing growth

they will manifest
their place in history
sands solidifying

an undying rock
I exit refusing
to be petrified

tracks too small
for the naked eye
trample my senses

my duty to decrypt
every footprint
each identity

I drink nectar
with native bees
they guide to nourish

red wattle birds
plant gardens and green
we adorn the earth

sometimes we sit
my soul and I

perched like birds
between soil and sky

when it flies down I follow
it follows me when I flit

it is how we get
to know each other

it is how we get
to grow each other

sometimes we sit
often it is just me

I am coming of age
I am intertidal

my new language
is petroglyph

an inhabited world
abraded bold

I trace my finger
join with nature

haematite
blood words

I play a prank
leave mystery here

meridians
mermaids

both are real
both fanciful

I am bowerbird
building a nest

magnetic
majestic

monogamous
polygynous

I am caught
courting myself

gathering twigs
and pebbles

experimenting
exploring

mandala
magical

wood turns serpent
in my hand

together we walk
rewinding the land

boulders push
sand slides

banks form
water flows

a prism slithers
towards us

every time I blink
a wildflower appears

such florid vision
stings my eyes

reverent
I meditate

this view is blinding
like temptation

I fear the beauty
I pine for it

I follow a matrix
of white shells

angry she kicks it
slumps on the sand

the crow flies off
her heart with him

parallel to dunes
I meander

whisks of grass
poke the air

we are fragile
windward

I smell sage
a prying lure

over the dunes
a world erupts

a horizon defined
creationism

a cathedral awaits me
the newest convert

I feel water flowing
from my head

I am drenched
as if baptised

when I ablute
there is blood

fearful I pray
curled into myself

a dingo appears
its eyes are wrens

red backed and fairy
I am purified

an astonishing stone
a footprint is there

my questions
prehistoric

who was here
how long ago

my answers
nostalgic

arriving to where
I'd always been

I am staring
at the new day

it grows brighter
and brighter

the sky and the sea
defined by blue

as if breathing now
the water is tidal

inhaling first
exhaling next

the horizon
a definition

I must define
my own horizon

arriving to shore
the painted land

leaving the ocean
I crave water

what joy is felt
when rain falls

the first time I see a cloud
I weep restated of mercy
volatile and fleet

the cloud weeps too
and within the rain I learn
I am at the mercy of self

after rain black mud
seeps between my toes

my pace is slowed
my tread heavy

I pause to rest
a rainbow appears

a reassuring delight
my heart is happy

as if a little child
has climbed inside

Blessing is nearby
I can feel her

on the skyline
Blessing is present

as I walk towards her
she does not move

as I embrace her
she fragments

now she is tree
and grass and air

now she is earth
and water and sky

the hills the mountains
the rivers and I

I am blessed to walk
amid the blessings

love is a daydream
filling with promise
a relentless mystery

there is no intimacy
caring of obligation
nor regret of deceit

this is the world
of the wildflowers
where joy exists

seek to find it
it is beside you
and inside you

the man bird arrives
returned to bird

the black of his cloak
is streaked with white

he chats incessantly
then warbles song

at first I am unhearing
not understanding

urgent he sings
head thrown back

as his throat vibrates
my eyes pulsate

if you see clearly
you will hear

if you hear loudly
you will see

a grain of sand
is a mountain

a drop of water
is the sea

listen strong
you are the song

my heart has become
a branch of a tree

birds visit me
to perch inside

no longer alone
I grow each day

my body fills
earth bound

my heart fills
sky bound

a porcupine offers quills
from his dying body
confronted I accept

gently he reassures
when death is near
we must give our beauty

when death is near
we must prepare
for the future

we lace a necklace
his death is dignity
as mine must be

the quill necklace
xylophones

story enters me
quills upon skin

my voice is born
fragile and soft

my voice grows strong
when I walk the land

a full moon
beams the landscape

everything ethereal
magic at the tips

on moist grass
I rest reclining

focus adjusts
astronomy

naked eyes
begin to trust

an emu appears
where life enters

I become orbital
pulled in

a flood plain
offers swans

like black rocks
they steer me

wetlands bloom
lily pink

brolgas dance
and chortle

their laughter
dissipates me

knee deep
I wade in

colour streams
aqua azure

sky reflects water
water reflects sky

the air in between
consumes me

I become vertigo
my mind distressed

shall I continue
or perish here

there is no way back
my past is blank

my future unseen
I am undefined

at night I sleep
and I am a child

black birds detour me
down into the earth

through sandstone veins
we descend tunnels

my eyes are strobed
wet blood now dry

inside this temple
I face my future

the air is musty
yet tastes sweet

inside the walls
a frieze of birds

the bones set
a winged strata

on the sandy floor
skeletons stretch

bone fingers inscribe
a sacred prayer

sound boomerangs
when they move

they are dancers
they are dancing

at night bones alight
a graveyard shines

skeletons dancing
the moon their smile

they are universal
yet only here

their eyes the stars
so all can see

nocturnal an owl arrives
silent flight fast and direct

how I envy its plumage
a masterpiece of art

it stares binocular
my eyesight grown

a new protocol
I am painted now

this is my totem
this is my song

resurrected
I stand in starlight

the landscape majestic
it is touching the sky

it is breathtaking
I inhale deeply

in every breath
the replica is love

when the moon is asleep
the Milky Way talks

stars raise me up
singing their names

Blessing is here too
she is a shooting star

born of cosmic fire
she shares her warmth

protected from the cold
I am lowered now

as I return to earth
ghosts walk beside me

the sky tilts east
it will be winter soon

from the cosmos
I learn my place

I am a boomerang
a fulcrum velocity

it is a humble task
so many before me

a lull and a doing
that is the journey

in the firmament
the heavens reveal

I am a solo candle
inside a chandelier

this is the wisdom
I need to succeed

my eyes adjust
I see the path
the path is song

do not diminish
the role of the mother

do not diminish
the role of the father

do not diminish
the role of the child

do not diminish
the role of the ant

the path is singing
my eyes adjust
I see the way

mountains in the distance
are a language I cannot read

mystery abounds there
along the cliff face

if you peer you will see
if you are deaf you will hear

if you are blind you will feel
legends inscribed here

an orange cliff
a ravine far below
a snake winding
womanly love
beautiful magnetic
spiritual expansive

my mother is risen
before my eyes

she is the mountain
yonder my father

a cloud spirit
forms an eagle

swooping us
encircling us

we are united
we are family

family inform me
water has memory
we carry aquifers
deep within us

I strip naked
at the waterhole
hold my breath
immerse my head

in this underworld
I see my offspring
softly defined
I reach for them

submerged
embryonic
perfection
not yet real

being present in the day
being part of the future

I return to the camp fire
gather handfuls of coals

toss up to the atmosphere
a ritual made of self

night falls immediate
embers become stars

from little they grow
akin to my heart

fire is medicine
it is my homeland

my house a bough shelter
built from ancient trees

in this crude dwelling
nests adorn all limbs

birds fan story here
an indelible sense of peace

when the owl dies
I gather it to me

brush dirt from its beak
wash its face and feathers

wrap gently in bark
lodge high in a tree

I pour my heart
into an open fire

dance the memories
praise the sorrow

it is an honour
to be honourable

I see her often
an old woman

she sings to birds
she sings to me

she turns to me
I see my reflection

I am born of her
she is the earth

responsibility returns
with her presence

in daylight the garden
is strewn with flowers

my mouth is a vase
for her wisdom

my body a vessel
for her welfare

I hear an echo echo echo
of a fallen tree

it will resonate forever
listen be forewarned

then it arrives
like a soft breeze
understanding

I have walked
through yesterday
through witnessing

ahead my future
fills with colour
my referendum

my hope crosses
from the previous
to the prophetic

in our creation
I am one page
not yet sanctified

I am one page
in a sanctified story
not quite genesis

Ali Cobby Eckermann is a poet and artist from South Australia whose work has been published and celebrated around the world. She is the author of six previous volumes of poetry including *Ruby Moonlight*, published by Magabala Books in Australia in 2012 and Flood Editions in North America in 2015. It was named the New South Wales Book of the Year and won the Kenneth Slessor Prize for Poetry, among other awards. She also published a memoir, *Too Afraid to Cry*, in 2012. In 2013 Ali toured Ireland as Australia's Poetry Ambassador, and in 2017 she received the Windham-Campbell Prize from Yale University. She describes herself as "a dreamer, a gardener, a reader and a nomad."